NELSON
MANDELA

Richard Tames

Franklin Watts

New York • London • Sydney • Toronto

Contents

© Franklin Watts 1991

Franklin Watts, Inc.
387 Park Avenue South
New York, N.Y. 10016

Phototypeset by: JB Type, Hove,
East Sussex
Printed in: Belgium
Series Editor: Hazel Poole
Designed by: Nick Cannan

Library of Congress Cataloging-in-Publication Data

Tames, Richard.
  Nelson Mandela/Richard Tames.
     p.   cm. — (Lifetimes)
  Includes bibliographical references and index.
  Summary: Describes the life and accomplishments of Nelson Mandela
from his early activities with the African National Congress to his
imprisonment and release.
  ISBN 0-531-14124-1
  1. Mandela, Nelson, 1918-   — Juvenile literature. 2. Civil
rights workers — South Africa — Biography — Juvenile literature.
3. African National Congress — Biography — Juvenile literature.
4. Political prisoners — South Africa — Biography — Juvenile
literature. [1. Mandela, Nelson, 1918-   . 2. Civil rights
workers. 3. African National Congress — Biography. 4. South Africa —
Biography.] I. Title. II. Series: Tames, Richard. Lifetimes.
DT1949.M35T36   1991
324.268'083'092 — dc20
[B]
[92]
                                                    90-43956
                                                    CIP
                                                    AC

"Stirring up trouble"

When Nelson Mandela was born, he was first given the Xhosa name Rolihlahla, which means "stirring up trouble." It is an apt name, as it describes the first half of his life when he devoted his great energies to organizing the struggle against apartheid. But his long-term goal has always been for a system of democracy which he believed would lead to peace between the different peoples of South Africa.

Nelson Mandela was born on July 18, 1918, in the family **kraal** at Qunu, a village in a fertile valley not far from Umtata, the most important settlement in the Transkei region. He was born into the royal family of his people, the Thembu, and was the son of the Paramount Chief's most senior adviser. In time he, too, might have expected to become a chief.

Mandela's early years were spent close to home. He helped by herding cattle on the communal farming lands of his people but he also went to a school run by missionaries. Even as a boy he learned that there were conflicting versions of his country's history. Around the fire at night, "the elders would tell tales about the wars fought by our ancestors in defense of the fatherland, as well as the acts of valor performed by generals and soldiers during those epic days." But in the books that he read in school, these same heroes were described as thieves and savages,

"The Great Place" — Mandela's birth-place in the Transkei.

while the white men were portrayed as brave pioneers in an empty land. When Mandela was 12-years-old, his father fell ill. He knew that he was dying and entrusted the upbringing of his son to the Paramount Chief, Jongintaba Dalindyebo. Mandela went to live with him at Mqekezweni, "the Great Place." He continued his schooling at Clarkebury, a nearby college, and from there he went on to Healdtown, a Methodist high school, and then to Fort Hare University College. There, he became involved in student politics and became good friends with another student, Oliver Tambo. When the powers of the Students' Representative Council were cut back, Mandela joined in the protests and was suspended.

The Paramount Chief ordered him to give up the protest and continue his studies. At the same

Walter Sisulu, who got Mandela to join the ANC; a prisoner 1963–89.

time, Mandela found out that the Chief had arranged a bride for him. He respected the traditions of his people, but education had given him new horizons and new ambitions. He was now 22-years-old and wanted to take charge of his own life. So he ran away to Johannesburg.

Johannesburg was a different world. A vast industrial city with great modern buildings, it was a striking symbol of South Africa's wealth and inequality. The whites lived in pleasant green suburbs, while the Africans were pushed out to overcrowded "locations," without proper roads, plumbing or electricity.

Tall and athletic, Mandela got a job as a guard at a mine. Then, thanks to a new friend, Walter Sisulu, who also came from Transkei, he was taken on by a firm of lawyers and began to study law part-time at the University of the Witwatersrand. Along with Sisulu, he also joined the African National Congress (ANC), an organization founded in 1912 to further the cause for democratic rights for South Africa's black people.

Shortly after joining the ANC in 1944, Mandela married Evelyn Ntoko Mase, a cousin of Sisulu. Her earnings as a nurse helped to pay for his law studies. Sisulu, Tambo and other younger members of the ANC felt that the organization was not definite enough in its actions. They wanted to infuse in the liberation movement "the spirit of African nationalism" and so the ANC Youth League was founded. In 1947, Mandela was elected as the Youth League's secretary, and in 1949 he became a member of the ANC's important National Executive committee.

He and other younger members wanted to organize a campaign against the new apartheid laws which caused increasing problems after the National Party came to power in South Africa in the 1948 general election. They planned a "Program of Action," which included strikes, **boycotts** and other nonviolent means to challenge the government.

But before they could launch their campaign, the South African

Mandela with his first wife, Evelyn, a nurse, who helped to finance his training as a lawyer. Their marriage was a casualty of his political commitment.

Communist Party, after having some of its leaders banned by the government, called for a strike in Johannesburg's mines on May 1, 1950. Mandela and the others were not pleased. Although some of the leaders of the Youth League were communists, there were always tensions in the ANC between them and the so-called Africanists like Mandela and Oliver Tambo, who was later to become the president of the ANC. Mandela and Tambo feared that the initiative for mass action had been taken from them. On May Day, more than half the miners stayed at home. Fights between strikers and strike breakers resulted in clashes with the police. Eighteen Africans were killed, some of them in group violence but most were apparently shot by police. Looking back, Mandela declared:

"That day was a turning point in my life, both in understanding through firsthand experience the ruthlessness of the police and in being deeply impressed by the support African workers had given to the May Day call."

Later that year, Mandela was elected National President of the Youth League. Throughout the following year, he and Sisulu worked out a new plan for mass action against unjust laws. Their campaign would be launched on April 6, 1952 — the day on which white South Africans would be celebrating the 300th anniversary of Dutch settlement. Nelson

Mandela was appointed to act as "Volunteer in Chief" of the "Defiance Campaign." On June 26, 1952, Mandela addressed a meeting in Johannesburg, which went on until after 11:00 p.m., the time when Africans were forbidden by law to be out without special passes, signed by a European. As he left the meeting, he was arrested. It was to be his first experience of imprisonment.

The effect of the Defiance Campaign was to make the South African government extend and strengthen the apartheid laws further. But it did also help to draw the attention of other countries to the situation in South Africa. At the same time it boosted membership of the ANC from 7,000 to over

The opening of the "Defiance Campaign" in June 1952. Note the presence of white and Indian allies.

100,000, making it a true mass organization for the first time.

Mandela was tried under the new "Suppression of Communism Act." This Act defined communism as any belief aiming to bring about change "by the promotion of disturbance or disorder."

He was found guilty but the judge noted that he and other leaders of the Defiance Campaign had repeatedly stressed the need to avoid violence. He was sentenced to nine months in prison, but the sentence was suspended for two years on condition that he did not repeat the offense.

African National Congress

The ANC was established to unite Africans regardless of tribe, language, religion or region, to fight for equal rights and to oppose domination by a white minority.

1912   Establishment of the ANC and adoption of its anthem Nkosi Sikelel' iAfrika (Lord Bless Africa).

1925   ANC adopts flag of black (for the people), green (for the land) and gold (for the resources).

1944   Formation of the Youth League.

1950   Defiance Program attracts mass membership.

1952   Chief Albert Lutuli elected president general of the ANC with Nelson Mandela as his deputy.

1959   Chief Lutuli calls for a boycott of South African goods.

1960   Pan Africanist Congress (PAC) splits off from ANC.
Unlawful Organization Act bans the ANC.
Chief Lutuli is awarded the Nobel Peace Prize.

1961   Formation of Umkhonto we Sizwe (Spear of the Nation) to back up ANC policy by military means.

1976   ANC supporting school children lead a countrywide protest against unequal education. Hundreds are killed in clashes with the police.

1984- A new constitution for the country
1986   introduced by the National Party government, giving limited rights to Asians and Coloreds but no rights to black people, results in countrywide revolt supported by the ANC.
The Western world, following pleas by the ANC, introduces **sanctions** against the government.

1985   South African business leaders meet ANC in Lusaka.

1987   Meeting between influential group of 50 Afrikaners and a senior representation of the ANC in Dakar, Senegal.

1988   ANC issues "Constitutional Guidelines for a Democratic South Africa."

1990   End of ban on ANC.
South African government starts official talks with the ANC on the prospects for a peaceful settlement of the country's political stalemate.

The ANC flag. Its colors symbolize the people (black), land (green) and resources (gold) of a country rich enough for all.

"Banned"

When Mandela was elected President of the Transvaal section of the ANC, the government immediately served him with a banning order which made it illegal for him to attend public meetings or to leave Johannesburg.

In 1952, Mandela qualified as a lawyer and set up in partnership with Oliver Tambo. As well as working as a lawyer, Mandela also lectured secretly to study groups in the African townships, although this was, of course, against the terms of his banning order. In 1953, almost as soon as his banning order ran out, it was renewed and he was forced to resign from the ANC. As

The "Congress of the People" at Kliptown, Johannesburg adopted the "Freedom Charter" enthusiastically as a program of wide appeal.

Oliver Tambo, Mandela's partner in legal practice, spent his exile representing the ANC internationally.

he pointed out, this was all because the South African government ordered it so — "without any hearing, without being faced by any charges."

As a banned person, Mandela was prevented from going to the "Congress of the People" organized in 1955 by the ANC and other anti-apartheid organizations. The 3,000 delegates enthusiastically adopted a "Freedom Charter" which was introduced by the ANC's National Executive. Although unable to attend, Mandela had been consulted about the Freedom Charter and could see why that and the occasion were so significant:

"Never before has any document or conference been so widely acclaimed and discussed by the democratic movement in South

The reforms demanded in 1955 were both political and economic and required an end to apartheid.

Africa. The Charter is more than a mere list of demands for democratic reforms; it is a revolutionary document precisely because the changes it envisages cannot be won without breaking up the economic and political setup of present South Africa."

As soon as Mandela's two year ban ran out a ncw one was imposed, this time for five years. The strain of police harassment and of trying to combine secret political activity with legal work began to have its effect on Mandela's marriage. His wife decided to train as a midwife and they were later divorced.

On December 5, 1956, Mandela was arrested in a dawn raid on his home and, along with Tambo, Sisulu and 153 others, was charged with high **treason**. Of the accused, 105 were African, 23 white, 21 Indian and 7 Colored. After a while they were granted bail, which meant that, when he was not actually needed in court, Mandela was free. Within the limits of his banning order, he kept up his legal practice, helping other people who were in trouble with the apartheid laws.

TREASON TRIAL

In good company — Mandela (middle of the third row up) towers head and shoulders over his co-defendants.

Nelson and his second wife, Winnie, on their wedding day, June 14, 1958. This marriage survived separation.

Mandela's trial was to last for over four years. It was during this time that he met Winnie Nomzamo Madikizela, a friend of Oliver Tambo's from his home village. She was young, beautiful and something of a celebrity — the first black medical social worker to be appointed at Baragwanath, a large African hospital. Her name, Nomzamo, means in Xhosa "someone who undergoes difficulties, someone who tries hard." Mandela saw in her a comrade for his political work as well as a partner for his private life and, once his divorce was final, they were married in 1958. Winnie soon became a member of the ANC's Women's League. When she joined a protest against the extension of the pass laws to women, she was imprisoned for a month and lost her job at the hospital as a result.

In 1959, a major dispute broke out in the ANC. A group calling themselves "Africanists" attacked the policy of cooperating with Indians and white communists and said they were using the ANC for their own ends. Led by Robert Sobukwe, a lecturer at the University of the Witwatersrand, they broke away to set up the Pan Africanist Congress (PAC).

In 1960, both the ANC and PAC organized nationwide protests against the pass laws and at Sharpeville, near Vereeniging, 5,000 unarmed protesters gathered outside a police station. A scuffle broke out and stones were thrown at the police. The 300 police officers present fired into the crowd, killing 69 people and wounding nearly three times as many. Another shooting incident took place at Langa, near Cape Town, on the same day.

The ANC responded by calling for strikes, marches and a national day of mourning. The United Nations Security Council blamed the South African Government for the bloodshed. The government declared a State of Emergency, banned the ANC and PAC and threw Mandela into prison along with 2,000 other opponents of the regime. By this time, Tambo had

left South Africa to set up ANC offices in exile in friendly parts of Africa and Europe.

The treason trial had, by now, been dragging on for three years but these dramatic events gave it a new interest. Mandela, a practicing lawyer, took over his own defense. His evidence and cross-examination filled 441 pages of the official court record.

The trial gave him the best opportunity he had ever had to declare publicly to South Africa and the world the basic policies of the ANC: "We are not antiwhite, we are against white supremacy." In March 1961, the court found Mandela and the other remaining accused not guilty.

Afterward — the Sharpeville massacre March 21, 1960.

Solidarity — supporters of the "Treason Trial" accused show their commitment.

Apartheid

"Apartheid" is an Afrikaans word meaning "separateness." It is a policy based on the idea that there are different and identifiable races who can and should be "developed" separately from one another. Under apartheid, the population is segregated into separate groups which are determined by color, language, descent and physical appearance. This classification dictates people's lives, their work, where they live, which schools they attend and whom they may marry.

The 1913 Native Land Act stopped Africans from buying land outside the rapidly diminishing areas under African communal **tenure** and the 1936 Natives' Representation Act in effect took away what limited vote they had. In 1948, the Afrikaaner-dominated Nationalist Party came to power.

Apartheid rapidly developed into a far-reaching system of control. The 1950 Population Registration Act classified people as Bantu (black), White or Colored (mixed race); later an Asian category was added. The Group Areas Act of the same year divided cities into areas reserved for each racial group. Other Acts banned strikes by African workers, enforced by law the custom of separate schools for blacks and whites, and made marriages between black and white people illegal.

In 1959, the Bantu Authorities Act was introduced with the intention of giving the various ethnic groups of the African population political rights in existing "Bantustans" (homelands). These Bantustans, of which the boundaries were fixed in 1936, wcre to be self-governing and eventually independent. Every African is assigned to a bantustan, mainly on the basis of language. The area set aside for bantustans covered less than 13 percent of the country and had to accommodate more than 70 percent of the population. In 1970, the Bantu Homelands Citizenship Act made every black South African a "citizen" of one of the bantustans, no matter where they actually lived. This made most blacks in South Africa foreigners in their own country.

In the 1980s, to meet international criticism, various forms of apartheid, such as the ban on mixed marriages, were abandoned. But the basis of the system, the enforced segregation of South Africans, still remains.

Rural idyll? On this Bantustan the work is being done by a woman and a boy using basic technology.

The Freedom Charter

"We, the people of South Africa, declare for all our country and the world to know: that South Africa belongs to all who live in it, black and white, and that no government can justly claim authority unless it is based on the will of the people ... The people shall govern; all national groups shall have equal rights; the people shall share in the country's wealth; the land shall be shared among those who work it; all shall be equal before the law; all shall enjoy equal human rights; there shall be peace and friendship ... the privacy of the house from police raids shall be protected by law ... all shall be free to travel without restriction ... the aged, the orphans, the disabled and the sick shall be cared for by the state ... the mineral wealth ... the banks and monopoly industry shall be transferred to the ownership of the people as a whole."

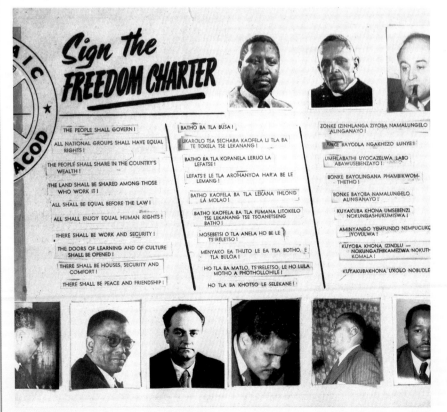

The "Freedom Charter" drawn up in 1955, summarizes a vision of a better future for all the peoples of South Africa.

"The Black Pimpernel"

Mandela's freedom was a victory but the ANC was now an illegal organization. It was decided that he should continue its work underground. For the next 17 months, he lived the life of a fugitive, seeing his family only occasionally, sleeping wherever a "safe house" would give him shelter, traveling disguised as a chauffeur or a window washer and constantly in fear of arrest. He became known as the "Black Pimpernel" after the daring and elusive master of deception in the novel *The Scarlet Pimpernel*, who defied the blood-thirsty government of revolutionary France in the 1790s.

In 1961, the other members of the Commonwealth forced South Africa to leave because it would not change its apartheid laws. The South African government drew up a new constitution which made the country a Republic and organized celebrations to mark the occasion. In the same year, Mandela was also doing his own organizing — mass protests to demand the calling of a National Convention to draw up a truly democratic constitution. In a secret interview with foreign journalists he warned that the ANC had pursued nonviolent methods for half a century and apartheid simply seemed to be getting stronger.

"If the government reaction is to crush by naked force our non-violent struggle, we will have to reconsider our tactics. In my mind we are closing a chapter on this question of a nonviolent policy."

Frustrated by their failure to force concessions by nonviolent means, the ANC leaders decided to set up a military wing — Umkhonto we Sizwe (Spear of the Nation) with Mandela in overall command. The two bodies would be quite separate, with the ANC continuing to confine itself strictly to nonviolent action. A small farm was rented at Rivonia, near Johannesburg, as a secret headquarters of Umkhonto. The new organization's main tactic would be sabotage, with the goal of destroying transportation and power facilities in order to damage the economy and discourage foreign investors from putting more money into South African industry. In this way, it was hoped to attract international attention to the cause and put pressure on the government without causing

Sabotage! Wrecked power lines disrupt industry and catch the headlines.

civilian casualties and thus creating bitterness which might take generations to heal.

In January 1962, Mandela was smuggled out of South Africa. In Ethiopia he addressed a Pan-African Freedom Conference. In London he met leaders of the British opposition parties to enlist their support, and in Algeria he undertook a course in military training. But, on August 5, 1962, soon after his secret return to South Africa, he was arrested by police following a tip-off and was imprisoned in the Johannesburg Fort.

Mandela was charged with organizing strikes and leaving the country without valid travel documents. Lacking any evidence, the authorities could make no accusations about his connection with Umkhonto. Conducting his own defense, Mandela emphasized that his actions had been essentially political rather than criminal and that he could scarcely expect a fair trial — "I am a black man in a white man's court." He was found guilty of both offenses and sentenced to five years imprisonment with hard labor. After serving some time sewing mailbags in Pretoria Central Prison, he was transferred to Robben Island, a maximum security prison seven miles off Cape Town.

In July 1963, police raided the farm at Rivonia, arresting Sisulu and seven others. Mandela was suddenly sent back to Pretoria Prison. In October, he and the others were charged with numerous offenses relating to the sabotage campaign. In stating his case, Mandela declared boldly that he had indeed helped to set up Umkhonto and had planned sabotage operations. It was true, he said, that communists had supported Umkhonto's efforts but that did not

Prisoners on Robben Island — breaking rocks (left) and sewing mailbags (right).

make him or his comrades communists themselves: "I have always regarded myself, in the first place, as an African Patriot ... " At the end of his four hour speech from the dock, Mandela concluded:

"I have fought against white domination, and I have fought against black domination. I have cherished the ideal of a democratic free society in which all persons live together in harmony and with equal opportunities. It is an ideal which I hope to live for and to achieve. But if needs be it is an ideal for which I am prepared to die."

The Rivonia Eight — Mandela, Sisulu, Mbeki, Mhlaba, Motsoaledi, Mlangeni, Kathrada and Goldberg.

While Mandela was Imprisoned

1963 United Nations calls for release of South African political prisoners.

1964 South Africa banned from Olympic Games.

1969 Protesters disrupt Springboks rugby tour of Britain.

1973 Organization of African Unity and Arab States impose oil boycott on South Africa.

1974 South Africa barred from General Assembly of the United Nations.

1977 Commonwealth adopts Gleneagles agreement banning sports events with South Africa.
Death of black **activist**, Steve Biko, in police detention.

1980 Umkhonto attacks Sasol coal-into-oil conversion plant.

1982 Umkhonto attacks Koeberg nuclear plant.

1984 Bishop Desmond Tutu awarded Nobel Peace Prize.

1985 Congress of South African Trade Unions established.
Chase Manhattan Bank stops loans to South Africa.

1986 Commonwealth Eminent Persons Group attempts to negotiate an end to apartheid.
Barclays Bank and Esso (Exxon) withdraw investments from South Africa.

1990 Namibia gains independence from South African occupation.

Steve Biko (1946–77), youth organizer who died in police custody.

Archbishop Tutu — an articulate international spokesman.

"The Prisoner"

Mandela was taken to Robben Island Maximum Security Prison and his "home" was a concrete cell seven feet square. His bed was a mat and two blankets and his uniform consisted of shorts and sandals, a shirt, jersey and thin jacket. The prisoners' regular diet was mostly corn mush, soup, black coffee and occasional portions of vegetables or meat. Every six months he would be allowed one letter of 500 words and a half hour visit, in which only family matters could be discussed.

Winnie, meanwhile, was issued with banning orders which cost her her job with the Child Welfare Department and prevented her from even taking her own children to school. In 1966, she was forbidden to write anything for publication and in 1969 she was arrested as a "suspected terrorist." Held for five months in solitary confinement, she was tried and acquitted. She was arrested again immediately and was tried and acquitted again seven months later. In all, she endured 491 days in solitary confinement. In 1974, she served another six months in prison for breaking the terms of her banning order.

Mandela — Prisoner No. 466/64 — continued to act as a leader, even in confinement. By organizing hunger strikes and go-slows, over the years the political prisoners won the right to better food, more

Still partners — Mandela and Sisulu on Robben Island in 1966, still struggling for their rights.

blankets, long pants, hot water for washing and facilities for sports and music. By keeping up his own daily routine of exercise and study, Mandela set an example of self-respect as well as physical and mental alertness. Forbidden access to any news, Mandela studied economics, improved his command of Afrikaans and taught law to his fellow prisoners.

In 1973, the Minister of Prisons offered to shorten Mandela's sentence if he would support the South African government's policy of making the Transkei an "Independent State." The offer was repeated several times. But Mandela knew that the policy of creating bantustans was simply a way of removing the African majority from any kind of control over the land and resources that rightly belonged to the whole

nation. His answer was always "No."

In June 1976, black school-children gathered in Soweto to protest against the government's bantu education policies which enforced the use of the Afrikaans language in schools. Police fired on the protesters, provoking further riots. More than 1,000 people, mostly young people, were killed over the following months. Thousands more fled over the border to join Umkhonto for military training.

Winnie Mandela led the way in voicing the outrage of the parents of those who had died and was punished with another five months in prison. In May 1977, she was banished, along with her daughter Zindzi, from her home in Soweto and sent to a location in Brandfort, 300 miles away. The three-room, concrete house assigned to her had

Soweto student uprising, 1976. The main demand was for an end to education in Afrikaans.

no water, no electricity and an outside bucket for a toilet. Every night and on weekends she was placed under house arrest.

In June 1980, the United Nations Security Council called on the

Also a prisoner — Winnie Mandela under house arrest.

Schoolboy Hector Petersen — first victim of the 1976 Soweto uprising. Hundreds more were to die.

South African government to release Mandela and other political prisoners to pave the way for "meaningful discussion of the future of the country." The South African government resisted any such idea but, for the first time, prisoners on Robben Island were allowed to receive newspapers and to buy groceries and toiletries with money earned from gardening. For Mandela and his comrades in the "special section," the worst days of hard labor, of road mending and seaweed gathering, were now over.

In April 1982, Mandela, Sisulu and three more Rivonia men were suddenly transferred to Pollsmoor Maximum Security Prison on the mainland, in a suburb of Cape Town. There they had more newspapers, access to radio and better food, but they were even more closely confined, without even a glimpse of the surrounding countryside.

Fighting back — a burning barricade in Athlone Township, Cape Town, during the 1985 disturbances.

In 1983, a new organization was established, the United Democratic Front (UDF), which brought together more than 600 separate organizations opposed to apartheid. The UDF pledged itself to support the Freedom Charter and elected Mandela as one of its patrons. It opposed the South African government's new **constitution** which wanted to form separate parliaments for whites, Indians and Coloreds and excluded Africans.

The year 1984 was a small milestone in terms of Mandela's imprisonment. He was allowed his first "contact" visit from Winnie. After 20 years, he could once more hold and kiss his wife.

In the outside world, the black townships rose in revolt against proposed rent increases. Between January 1984 and July 1986, more than 2,000 people were killed in an apparently unstoppable cycle of revolt and repression.

In January 1985, Mandela was visited by the South African Minister of Justice, H.J. Coetsee, accompanied by Lord Bethell, a British Conservative and Member of the European Parliament. The visit was meant to provide independent confirmation that Mandela was being well treated and was in good health. Bethell was greatly impressed by Mandela's relaxed dignity and awareness of current world politics. On January 27, The *Mail on Sunday* newspaper gave a full account of Lord Bethell's visit to Pollsmoor. It hailed Mandela as "the undisputed leader of the black population of South Africa," condemned "the vile policy of apartheid" and declared that it "unhesitatingly joins all those throughout the world, of whatever political persuasion, who cry the slogan, 'Release Mandela Now!' " This showed the widespread international condemnation which the South African government now had to face.

Honors for Nelson Mandela

A larger than life bust of Mandela at London's South Bank arts complex, one of many worldwide tributes.

* *International Prizes, Honors and Awards*
  Jawaharlal Nehru Award for International Understanding (India 1979).
  Dr. Bruno Kreisky Prize for Human Rights (Austria 1981).
  Simon Bolivar Prize (Venezuela 1983).
  Playa Giron Award (Cuba 1984).
  Star of International Friendship (German Democratic Republic 1984).
  Third World Prize (Great Britain 1985).
  W.E.B. Dubois International Medal (United States 1986).
  Alfonso Comin Foundation Peace Award (Spain 1986).
  International Peace and Freedom Award (Sweden 1986).
  Third World Prize (Malaysia 1986).
  Bremen Solidarity Prize (Federal Republic of Germany 1988).
  Nominated for Nobel Peace Prize 1986 and 1987.
* Freedom of the cities of Glasgow, Rome, Olympia, Aberdeen, Florence, Sydney and Wijnegen (Belgium).
* Honorary degrees from the universities of Lancaster, Lesotho, Zimbabwe, Havana, Michigan and Brussels (Free University) and from the City College of New York and the Ross University Medical School.
* Streets have been named after Mandela in Dakar (Senegal), Gaberones (Botswana), Glasgow and in London. In other areas of Great Britain there are parks, as well as housing and a public building bearing his name; in the German Democratic Republic there is a school named after him and in the French city of Grenoble a square. In London and Dublin there are public monuments as well.

"Free Mandela"

On January 31, 1985, State President P.W. Botha told the South African House of Assembly that the government was willing to consider Mandela's release if he would **renounce** the ANC's use of violence and "conduct himself in such a way that he will not again have to be arrested." Botha argued that "it is therefore not the South African government which now stands in the way of Mr. Mandela's freedom. It is he himself. The choice is his." Mandela gave his reply at a mass meeting in Soweto, read out by his daughter Zindzi. It was his first direct public statement in twenty years:

"I am not a violent man ... It was only then when all other forms of resistance were no longer open to us that we turned to armed struggle ... Only free men can

A special messenger – Zindzi Mandela passes on her father's words, 1985.

negotiate. Prisoners cannot enter into contracts ... I cannot and will not give any undertaking at a time when I and you, the people, are not free. Your freedom and mine cannot be separated. I *will* return."

In February, Oliver Tambo urged the people of the townships to make South Africa ungovernable. The ANC was increasingly confident that the South African authorities were cracking: "The future is within our grasp." Protests grew more

Failing to grasp the nettle — State President P.W. Botha.

violent and the police response more ruthless. In July 1985, a State of Emergency was declared. The number of people killed continued to rise into the hundreds. International pressure mounted to impose economic sanctions on South Africa to force the government into abolishing apartheid. France and the United States took the lead. It is estimated that between 1985 and 1989 these sanctions cost South Africa betwen $32 billion and $42 billion. Meanwhile, the ANC's "Freedom" radio stations in Lusaka and Addis Ababa urged people to make weapons and gasoline bombs to fight back against the security forces. The United States Secretary of State, George Shultz, called for the release of Mandela and for

negotiations with the ANC "before it is too late."

In 1986, the Commonwealth Group of Eminent Persons, a delegation of seven leading politicians, made three visits to Mandela and reported on his "immaculate appearance, his apparent good health and his commanding presence." They, too, urged Botha to negotiate with the ANC. In May 1988, the 42nd session of the United Nations General Assembly likewise called for Mandela's unconditional release.

Mandela, himself, wrote to President Botha to sketch out a path forward:

"The key to the whole situation is a negotiated settlement, and a meeting between the government and the ANC will be the first major step towards peace in the country."

Mandela saw two major questions to be dealt with — the demand for majority rule in a single, undivided South Africa and the need to reassure whites that "majority rule will not mean domination of the white minority by blacks." He concluded:

"I believe that the overwhelming majority of South Africans, black and white, hope to see the ANC and the government working closely together to lay the foundation for a new era in our country in which racial discrimination and prejudice, **coercion** and confrontation, death

Party for an absent guest — 70th birthday celebration for Mandela.

and destruction, will be forgotten."

In July 1988, 75,000 people filled London's Wembley Stadium for a concert in honor of Mandela's 70th birthday. It was broadcast to 64 countries and seen by a billion people. At Mandela's house in Soweto, 11 mailbags of cards from well-wishers were delivered.

A month later, it was revealed that Mandela had been transferred to the hospital for treatment for **tuberculosis**. Calls for his release took on a new urgency, as fears for his health increased. As he recovered, he was transferred to a bungalow in the Victor Verster Prison Farm at Paarl, near Cape Town.

In July 1989, President Botha, on the verge of resignation after years of trying hopelessly to preserve apartheid while appearing to reform it, had a brief meeting with Mandela. Both men agreed to "confirm their support for peaceful developments in South Africa." In September 1989, F.W. de Klerk became president and was determined to break out of what he called "the cycle of violence." He found Mandela ready to listen but firmly sticking to his principles. The world's most famous political prisoner was, in effect, dictating the conditions of his own release.

On October 15, 1989, Walter Sisulu and seven other political prisoners were released to a tumultuous welcome. On December 13, de Klerk and Mandela met face to face. Mandela declared that the president was "the most serious and honest white leader he had come across." On February 2, 1990, de Klerk announced the end of the ban on the ANC, PAC, Communist Party and over 30 antiapartheid organizations and on February 11, 1990, Nelson Mandela walked out of prison, a free man for the first time in over 27 years.

On the day of his release, Mandela proclaimed confidently that "Today the majority of South Africans, black and white, recognize that apartheid has no future." At immense rallies and in numerous

Finding a way forward — State President F.W. de Klerk.

28

Free at last! Mandela's warmth and dignity at once impressed all who met him.

interviews he repeated his call for an end to the State of Emergency and the release of all political prisoners, for the maintenance of international sanctions, and for the armed struggle to remain as a defensive strategy only as long as apartheid itself was upheld by violence.

Mandela emerged from prison calm and dignified, with a natural air of authority and, as one British journalist reported, "His presence quite simply overshadows everyone who is in his company." In the days following his release, Mandela addressed several rallies, each time speaking with calm and reasoned logic and showing no sign of vengeance or hatred. Chris Hani, deputy commander of Umkhonto declared: "I think we're going to learn from him that we need to be better South Africans — to forgive and forget and to look forward to building a new South Africa." For his own part, however, Mandela denied that he was any kind of prophet come to lead the nation from the wilderness. Many hoped that he would prove to be a guide, even though he had quoted India's founder, Nehru, on several occasions to warn that there would be "no easy walk to freedom ..."

Find out More

Important Books

Higher Than Hope: The Biography of Nelson Mandela by Fatima Meer (Harper & Row, 1989)

Mandela by Ronald Harwood (State Mutual Book, 1988)

Nelson and Winnie Mandela by Dorothy and Thomas Hoobler (Franklin Watts, 1987)

Part of My Soul Went With Him by Winnie Mandela (Norton, 1985)

The Struggle is My Life (rev. ed.) by Nelson Mandela (Path Press, 1986)

Important Dates

1918 Born at Qunu, near Umtata, Transkei

1930 Becomes ward of Paramount Chief

1940 Goes to Johannesburg

1944 Joins ANC and marries Evelyn Ntoko Mase

1947 Becomes Secretary of ANC Youth League

1950 Elected National President of Youth League

1952 Leads "Defiance Campaign" as Volunteer in Chief and is arrested

1953 Forced to resign from ANC

1956 Elected Deputy President of ANC and charged with treason

1958 Marries Winnie Nomzano Madikizela

1960 Detained under State of Emergency regulations

1961 Acquitted of treason Heads Umkhonto we Sizwe and goes underground

1962 Tours Africa and visits London

Arrested and sentenced to five years hard labor

1963 Charged with sabotage

1964 Sentenced to life imprisonment

1973 Refuses reduction of sentence in return for supporting bantustan policy

1982 Transferred to Pollsmoor Prison

1983 Elected patron of the UDF

1985 Refuses release in return for denouncing armed struggle

1986 Meets Commonwealth Group of Eminent Persons

1988 Honored by 70th Birthday concert at Wembley, London

1989 Meets Presidents Botha and F.W. de Klerk

1990 Released from prison Elected Deputy President of ANC Leads ANC team in preliminary talks on negotiations with South African government End of State of Emergency

Important Addresses

African-American Institute
833 United Nations Plaza
New York, N.Y. 10017

African National Congress of South
  Africa
801 Second Avenue
New York, N.Y. 10017

Glossary

Activist   Somebody who actively supports certain policies and helps to strengthen the support of political ideas.

Boycott   The act of refusing to take part in dealings in order to force another party to change its actions or policy.

Coercion   Being held back and restrained by force or the threat of force.

Constitution   Basic law governing the structure of government.

Kraal   South African village of huts usually surrounded by a fence.

Pioneers   People who are among the first to build and develop a new land.

Renounce   To publicly reject and disown.

Sanctions   Military or economic measures taken by a country in order to persuade another to follow a set course of action.

Tenure   Conditions on which property is held.

Treason   Betrayal of the state.

Tuberculosis   A disease of the lungs, often caused by bad living conditions, which can be fatal.

Index

Picture Acknowledgements

The publishers would like to thank the International Defense and Aid Fund for South Africa for their kind permission to reproduce their photographs in this book.